Speech Therapy for Toddlers:

An essential guide on how to develop early communication skills for your kids

Dr. Debbie Bryan

Table of contents

Chapter 1

Early contacts skills and why they are crucial

Before youngsters begin to communicate they need to build their early communication abilities. These include: gazing, shared attention, taking turns, and listening. These abilities are crucial building blocks for improving understanding and communication. A lot of critical communication abilities develop before the first words arrive.

Children need you! They require chances to speak with familiar adults. Children communicate more when people react to their communication efforts, however, and whatever they have said. It may be via smiles, gestures, presenting and offering items, pointing, and making noises.

Look for chances to communicate with your kid; anything may be an occasion for chatting and playing with them. This will assist kids to learn about communication and start strengthening those communication abilities.

6 Early Social Skills in Children and How to Improve Them

Social skills are critical for early childhood development. From eye contact to turn-taking, these social skills help youngsters communicate, create and sustain relationships, manage their emotions, and more.

Helping your toddler become socially competent is vitally crucial for healthy childhood development. It's how kids learn to navigate the world around them, build healthy relationships with classmates, adults, and instructors, and even contribute to their academic achievement.

There's a tendency to imagine that social skills evolve spontaneously by simply placing youngsters in social situations. And although this is undoubtedly part of the process, the basis for building good social talents begins with early interactions with their parents and loved ones.

Just as your child's early communication abilities begin long before your child's first words, early social skills develop before youngsters join the school or even daycare.

Children are social novices, and they look to their caregivers as role models on how to act and respond in various circumstances. They monitor, learn, and absorb the social activities and interactions of adults around them. At an early age, you're the largest influence in your kid's life, and you have emotional and cognitive capabilities to assist your child to develop their social skills. How you share this information with your kid can eventually benefit them for a lifetime!

In this post, we're going to break down some crucial early social skills and give advice on how to enhance these abilities with your little one throughout the day. Spending 20-30 minutes each day with your kid will not only enable them to enhance their social and linguistic abilities but also teach them the nonverbal fundamentals required for healthy communication.

What are the advantages of early social skills?

We hone and strengthen social abilities throughout our lives. But this adventure starts from the time your kid is born!

Here are a few of the important advantages of helping your kid acquire good social skills:

- Understanding and paying attention to social signals, such as body language and tone of voice
- Coping with large emotions, such as anger or grief, in a socially suitable manner
- Recognizing and empathizing with other people's feelings
- Considering other people's ideas or opinions
- Finding effective strategies to overcome conflict
- Forming and sustaining partnerships and friendships
- Forgiving others and showing contrition

Eye Contact

Eye contact is one of the earliest social skills you may see in your kid. It's also one of the earliest bonding moments you have with your infant, making you both feel more connected to one other. This capacity to sustain constant eye contact should begin around 2-3 months.

So why is eye contact so important? It develops a connection with another individual and displays that we are listening and attentive. We utilize eye contact in so many regular encounters throughout the day, from chatting with friends to conversing with receptionists or checking out our groceries. Without making eye contact, spoken communication may seem awkward and lead to unpleasant situations.

Here are a few fun and easy exercises to focus on establishing and prolonging eye contact with your young child:

- Make a ridiculous face at each other
- Sing to your baby
- Play a game of peek-a-boo
- Make ridiculous noises together

Joint Attention

Joint attention occurs when two persons are concurrently focused on the same thing, person, or activity. It's one of the most critical talents required to build good social and linguistic skills.

Let's take the basic act of bouncing a ball with your toddler. If they're not paying attention to the ball, they won't be able to actively engage in the game. In reality, to acquire most new abilities, youngsters have to be focused on the object or instruction of another person. Otherwise, it'll be practically hard for them to reproduce similar duties in the future.

Establishing shared attention is also one of the antecedents of the back-and-forth flow of communication. When we communicate with other people, we're both engaged on the topic at hand. It helps each individual listen, pay attention, and answer relevant questions.

For instance, if you point to an item and tell your kid, "look at that!" you would expect your youngster to tilt their head to look at the thing. This may lead to a natural discussion where your youngster finally answers questions and offers their perspective.

The good news is that there are so many ways you can assist your kids to increase joint attention throughout their everyday lives.

One easy action that you may already be doing is singing with your kid. Even if your kid isn't yet singing along with words, are they gazing at you and smiling? This is a beautiful symbol! During songs, one strategy to boost their attention and get kids engaged is to leave a sentence open-ended.

You may say something like, "Old McDonald had a farm—-" and then wait for your youngster to finish the term with

"E-I-E-I-O." Maybe your toddler will retain eye contact and wait anxiously for you to continue the statement. Or maybe they'll finish it for you! Either way, both of you are focusing on the same music at the same moment.

Reading is another fantastic shared attention activity. While a toddler may not comprehend the subtleties of a tale, pointing to images in a book and identifying items helps them concentrate their attention. For instance, you may remark, "Oh wow.

Look at that massive train! Choo choo!" If your youngster doesn't appear to be paying attention, don't be hesitant to grasp their hand and point to the image you're describing. Try choosing one photo on each page. Making this part of their nap or sleep routine not only helps with joint attention but helps create pre-literacy abilities as well.

As we noted previously, playing with a ball is also a simple, effective joint attention exercise. First, show your youngster the ball and then create eye contact. You may create anticipation with "ready, set...go!"

Back and Forth Vocalization

Long before you hear your child's first wonderful words, they'll begin to create plenty of expressive noises. This might include cooing, babblings, and other verbalizations.

In the first 3 months, kids will often begin to coo and gurgle and you could even hear their first chuckle. These are the early phases of communication when newborns start to explore with their voices. Around 3-6 months, a baby will begin to produce more vowel sounds. You could even start to hear their first consonants such as "bababa."

During this stage of communication development, you should begin engaging in back-and-forth vocalizations with your kid. This is when your kid will try to replicate a sound that you generate or perhaps begin a sound for you to repeat.

These noises are not always self-directed but are designed to make a connection between you and others. Your baby is starting to comprehend the cause-and-effect of communication - first, you say something, then they reply, and so forth. This is a significant communication milestone!

Children learn by mimicking people around them. That's why it's never too early to start working on back-and-forth vocalizations with your tiny one.

To encourage your infant to mimic, try making basic noises, such as "Aaah" and "oooh." Play around with your loudness and intonation, and be sure to utilize exaggerated facial expressions. This will not only capture your baby's attention but also enhance their probability of replicating your noises.

You may also practice targeting ambient noises, such as automobiles (vroom, beep beep) and animal sounds (meow, woof woof) (meow, woof woof). As we indicated previously, pointing to certain items in books and making these noises may boost both joint attention and their back and forth vocalizations.

Finally, get in front of a mirror! Kids adore being ridiculous, so make funny expressions, exaggerate noises, and sing songs. Establishing eye contact and shared attention in the mirror helps keep your toddler interested and creates possibilities to copy your vocalizations.

Imitation of Play

Imitation isn't simply the greatest form of flattery, it's also how we learn. And it applies to fun as well.

Playing is one of the most crucial components of early childhood development. It's how youngsters improve their social and linguistic skills, problem solve, learn how to share and take turns, and comprehend their surroundings.

Using Play to Promote Speech & Language Development
Play is a vital aspect of learning in children. It helps children explore and comprehend their world, stimulate language development, problem solve, gain social skills, and so much more!

However, not all youngsters instinctively or independently find out how to play successfully or interact with a new item. They typically need help to perform a task, such as stacking blocks. This becomes increasingly more true when toddlers utilize more difficult toys, such as solving a puzzle or exploring sensory activities like play-dough.

When a youngster eventually does figure out how toys function, they begin to grasp cause and effect. If they stack the blocks too high, the blocks can fall as a consequence. If they push a toy vehicle, it will drive on the track where they want it to go. The back and forth nature of communication follow the same norms of cause and effect.

Between the ages of 18 and 24 months, youngsters will start to develop their pretend play abilities and begin utilizing objects for their original purpose.

For instance, instead of merely slamming toys together or mouthing them, kids can like pretending to cook in a kitchen or feeding a plush animal. These are fantastic exercises to build on the language and social skills.

If your kid is feeding their baby doll a bottle, add some linguistic signals such as "yum" or "ooh, it's hot!"

If you're playing with your kid in their toy kitchen, describe their activities such as "stir" or "turn on the oven."

If your youngster is chatting on a toy phone, say things like "hello" and "who is this?"
Take time out each day to get down on the floor, play with your kid, and as they become older, use toys responsibly. Give your kid lots of examples of what you'd want them to see, do, and copy.

Turn-Taking

Effective communication involves the capacity to take turns. When one person speaks, the other waits and listens then answers. If we didn't allow this turn-taking to happen, our conversational partners could disconnect or feel annoyed. Likewise, if youngsters have problems with turn-taking, they could constantly interrupt others, talk without taking a break, or not actively listen.

These abilities are built early when youngsters learn how to take turns sharing toys with their family and friends. Many parents will tell that one of their child's first words is "mine." With little effort, this may grow into "my turn."

Many of the basic exercises we covered above build the framework for turn-taking. You can build turn-taking into stacking blocks, putting together a puzzle, moving a vehicle back and forth, or pretty much any activity that involves two players! Make sure to use motions to point out "my turn" and "your turn" to assist your toddler to understand that patience is essential for turn-taking to happen.

Sharing

If your youngster is starting to comprehend the notion of turn-taking, the next stage is learning how to share.

This social ability isn't only vital at home (particularly if they have siblings), but at school and at pretty much every point during a person's life.

A youngster always wants things instantly. However, they might have to wait their turn or, even better, ask permission to share the desired toy. It also helps kids develop ties with family and classmates and learn to relate to others.

Because children learn via imitation, it is crucial to establish a model of sharing within the household.

Share a snack with your youngster and say "Here you go. I adore sharing because it makes everyone happy!" Use positive reinforcement and offer your youngster feedback throughout the day to strengthen this ability.

A simple technique to develop sharing is by practicing with siblings or friends. For instance, offer your kid a toy and explain that they may share the object with their sibling or take turns using it. If they have difficulties grasping this idea, add a visual signal such as a timer and set it for 5 minutes. Each kid then gets to play with the toy for 5 minutes, ensuring that everyone has a chance.

Using prizes, such as a sticker system, may also assist a youngster get motivated to share. While many parents use this technique for potty training, it's also a fantastic way to develop early social skills. Every time your child successfully shares, they get a sticker. And once they receive 10 stickers, they get some type of reward - maybe a favorite treat or some extra playtime.

We've covered a ton of important early social skills and how to improve them with your child. And you may already be implementing these strategies with your child at home today. Keep up the great work!

The social skills your child learns in early development will help them establish and maintain strong connections with family and peers (and eventually spouses, colleagues, and employers) (and eventually spouses, colleagues, and employers). They'll become more socially adept and prepared once they enter school.

If you're still concerned about your child's social skill development, speak with your pediatrician or a speech-language pathologist. This is the first step in helping you and your child work on these early building blocks of communication.

Why are Early interactions skills important?

The advantages will have a lasting influence on the kid and by making sure that they are given an opportunity for social contact early, it is ensured that the child will have a firm foundation for their social abilities as they develop and ultimately become an adult. By choosing a childcare provider which emphasizes social connection early, a kid may obtain the following benefits:

- Learning to Work with Others

Teamwork is a talent that will be helpful throughout life, and it is centered on the concepts of sharing, communicating, compromising, and working towards shared objectives. As youngsters play together in controlled learning situations such as child care, they will begin to comprehend the necessary methods for interacting effectively with others.

- Developing Communication Skills with Child Care

While early communication skills are developed by imitating adults, children also need to learn to communicate verbally with peers. Social interaction from an early age is a key factor in learning to speak effectively for clear communication. Through communication with others at places like child care, kids also gain a sense of self and learn to identify as individuals, which is a normal part of the developmental process for toddlers.

- Understanding Social Cues

Non-verbal communication is another important component of social interaction for children. As kids play and learn together, they will begin to understand emotions expressed through facial expressions and body language. Not only will this be valuable in knowing what others are feeling, but it is also helpful for children who are just learning to express themselves.

- Building friendships

Friendships are crucial for young children, and they are only developed via frequent social contacts. Because children do not have innate problem solving and conflict resolution skills at young ages, guided social interactions help forge friendships that will be necessary for building confidence and self-esteem.

Should all children be given the same amount of social interaction?

Things aren't always so straightforward. Just like in the adult world no two children are the same. They will all have varying degrees of comfort as well as delight in how they handle social settings. Children that are more introverted for example may benefit and receive greater delight from less social engagement than other children.

They may find it more comfortable to just have 2 or 3 close pals rather than being part of a bigger group. On the other side, more extroverted children may like being among their peers for longer periods and may enjoy themselves more in a greater group.

Additionally, it is also vital to address the requirements of children who may have a mental health conditions such as autism spectrum disorder. These children may have a very challenging time in social circumstances and special attention should be taken in aiding these children to enable them to engage with people in a manner that still allows them to feel secure and comfortable.

Chapter 2

Fun activities and strategies to develop interpersonal skills for Toddlers

What you need is a huge stack of varied activities — physical, sensory, arty, creative, surprise, messy, or just plain stupid – to pick from throughout the day, depending on your toddler's mood and energy levels. So, we've come up with 26 tried-and-tested activities — some of which take a little prep and others which need no prep at all – for you to have up your toddler-entertainment sleeve. Have fun!

Here's our list of the finest games you can play with your toddler inside

1. Follow my leader
Get your kid has to replicate everything you do: leaping, crawling, stroking your stomach, placing your slippers on your head

- the sillier the better! Then it's her time to lead...

2. Rescue the animals
Gather together some toy animals (or automobiles or little dolls) and a roll of masking tape. Use strips of masking tape to glue the toy animals, one by one, to a window or a door.

Then urge your youngster to 'rescue' the toys by gently peeling/pulling off the tape. It's a fun game for toddlers that's particularly useful for improving fine motor skills and hand-eye coordination. And MadeForMums superuser Abi, who submitted this image of her daughter Maisie enjoying the game, said Maisie also liked re-sticking the animals back on the glass and asked Mum to save them for round 2!

3. Hunt for hidden riches
You'll need some little toys and sand for this one – either sandpit sand or, if you don't

have any, you can manufacture super-quick play sand (with flour and oil) (with flour and oil). Put the sand in a washing-up basin and conceal the toys in it. Give your youngster a spoon and a sieve and start them out 'hunting for treasures'. (You may wish to lay a mat/sheet on the floor beneath the bowl to collect any errant shoveled grains.)

4. Play Parcel Surprise

Use some old paper to wrap up a couple of your child's favorite toys (don't use too much sticky glue). Then give one package to your kid and ask them to guess what's inside - is it Teddy? Or Dolly? Or Panda? Then let your youngster unwrap the item (OK, rip off the paper) and experience the thrill of finding out.

5. Sweep and dust

Toddlers adore emulating grown-ups by performing the mundane home activities that most of us grown-ups would happily do without. So, give your toddler a soft cloth and begin 'dusting' together. Or grab them a little broom or dustpan and brush – or even one of the little toy vacuum cleaners that make fantastic, important-sounding suction sounds – and spend some time getting the floor all spick and span.

6. Do some magic painting
Draw a simple pattern on paper with a white candle or crayon. Make up watery paint in a bold shade and let your child paint the paper. As they color the paper, it will unveil the 'magic' concealed pattern.

7. Play musical bumps
You don't need to be at a party to play a basic, giggly version of this game. Play some music and dance about together, assuring your youngster that you're both going to sit down as soon as the music stops. Then hit pause on the music and yell, "Quick, sit down!" Once your child's got the hang of the game, make sure you're a little dozy and sluggish at sitting down periodically, so that

they have a chance to feel good about beating you to it.

8. Pretend to be animals
Draw an animal's face on a piece of card or, if the drawing's not your thing, print one off (there are several wonderful ones to download at Twinkl) and cut holes for the eyes. Let your youngster paint it, then put a straw to the bottom so they can hold it in front of their face. Make many masks and take it in turns to pretend to be the various creatures, with plenty of moving about on all fours and growling/quacking/bleating sounds.

9. Play postie
Posting items into various shaped holes fascinates toddlers and may keep them occupied for hours. And the action of posting is fantastic for developing fine motor skills (grasping an item, putting it over a hole, and letting go) and also knowing that when you drop something into

a container it doesn't go away. Try one of the 8 various posting activities parent and primary school teacher, Kate, outlines on YouTube that involve ordinary household goods, such as milk cartons, cardboard boxes, and present bags.

10. Get potato printing
This is one of those hobbies that babies enjoy but many of us avoid because, honestly, who's got time to carve a reverse 3-D pattern into a potato? Well, we have a wonderful trick! All you need is cookie cutters (and a potato or two, obvs), and then...

With a knife, cut a potato in half vertically, then push a cookie-cutter directly into one of the sliced surfaces – so that you can just barely see the top of the cookie cutter.
Take your knife and make an incision into the side of the potato half about where the implanted end of the cookie-cutter is. Stop

when you feel your knife contact the cookie cutter.

Cut around the remainder of the side of the potato half in the same manner.
Peel off the strip of potato you've just cut, leaving the central part (within the cookie-cutter) in place.
Remove the cookie cutter – and you have a nicely formed potato stamper!

Put some poster paint in saucers and let your youngster dip the potato in the paint and then draw prints on paper. Alternatively, an older child might brush paint onto the potato stamper with a paintbrush before stamping.

11. Make a toy garage
With a cardboard box, some loo roll or kitchen roll tubes, scissors, and adhesive tape, you can make this handmade toy-car garage for toddlers, which we first discovered when it was shared by mom

Leanna Bannister on the Family Lockdown & Tips Facebook page. How to manufacture it? Leanna tells us:

"I just put a baby wipes box on its side, taped several cardboard rolls together, and slipped them inside the box! My kid Vinnie hasn't let it alone since he's got it! He likes taking all the cars out, then figuring out which vehicles can go in certain tubes! So easy to prepare and hours of fun!"

12. Walk like a bear

In this action game, you and your kid have to move about the room like one of the 7 members of the 'Bear Family' (you call out which one) (you call out which one). And each of them walks in distinct ways. So for:

Papa Bear – take BIG leaps
Mama Bear – take modest steps
Baby Bear – take little steps
Brother Bear – bounce around
Sister Bear – jump on one foot
Polar Bear – walk on all fours

Sleepy Bear - cuddle up on the floor and snore

Start with only 2 of the Bear Family and build up until your child can recall all 7 and their distinct behaviors.

13. Do the washing up

Not the actual washing up. But you can have a lot of splashy fun with a plastic toy tea set or plastic beakers, plates and silverware, a sponge, and a (half-full) basin of warm soapy water. You can't even begin to think you'll play this game and keep dry but you can't stop a genuine flood with a splash mat, an apron (for both of you), and lots of tea towels to place cleaned objects on.

14. Slot the sticks

A little step up from simple 'posting through holes', this is a brilliant activity, shared with us by MadeForMums superuser Amy, for further developing an older toddler's fine-motor skills – it's harder to post objects through small slots than bigger holes and the action requires using the wrist as well as the hands. You'll need some lollipop sticks (painted in bright colors, if possible) and a big container with a plastic top (that you don't need anymore).

Use scissors or a knife to gently cut a few tiny slits across the lid. Check if the slots are broad enough to accommodate a lolly stick-through. Then demonstrate to your youngster how to fit a lolly stick through the opening and let them have a try. Amy's made her slots a good deal thicker than her lolly sticks but you can ratchet up the challenge by making them narrower or even simply cutting lolly-stick-width slits.

15. Create a huge collage
Collect collected various bits and pieces of different sizes and textures – such as candy wrappers, shreds of cloth, bits of foil, cotton wool, feathers, drawings of animals or flowers cut from magazines or pamphlets, and yogurt pot lids. Tape a big square of

sticky-backed plastic to a window or door, sticky-side facing out. If you don't have any sticky-backed plastic, you may put up some lines of adhesive tape (sticky side facing out) instead. Give your youngster a bowl holding all the bits and pieces and let them start stuck.

16. Sieve pasta

This is a super-simple one. Put some dry spaghetti (all one shape or a mix of various forms) into a huge plastic bowl. Hand your youngster a plastic jug or spoon and a sieve for plenty of scooping, gathering, sorting, and pouring.

17. Hold a toy tea party

Spread down a mat or sheet on the floor and bring all your child's favorite toys over for a tea party. Give everyone their plastic cups or beakers and plates. Put some play food or little triangles of bread or cake on a bigger plate and encourage your child to offer the toys something to eat.

If you have a plastic jug or teapot, you may give juice or tea, too – but make that pretend juice or tea or you'll be spending all your time in spillage-control mode. Talk with your youngster about which meals the toys enjoy (and don't like) and what the toys are conversing about. Don't forget to tell the toys to say please and thank you — and to share generously!

18. Roll the ball
Any softball will be fine for this activity but remember that your youngster will find it easier the larger the ball is. Get your youngster to sit on the floor with her legs spread, while you do the same — seating opposite them, so your feet are touching.

Place the ball on the floor in front of you and roll it to your kid, urging them to 'catch it' (which is stopping it with their hands) and then roll it back to you. You may add added excitement to the game by repeating a goofy term, such as "Eeep!" as you roll, and encourage your kid to repeat the "Eeep!" when they roll it back. Change the sound after a few rolls each.

19. Do some flour drawing
This is a beautiful sensory exercise but it is a dirty one - so be ready with splash mats and a dustpan and brush. MadeForMums superuser Sarah, who's posted her image of her 2-year-old daughter Orla doing some flour sketching, was amazed by how long Orla spent on this activity. "I threw some flour out on a board and handed her a chopstick and she made designs in it.

 She was entertained for at least 20 minutes and extremely satisfied simply drawing!" For a somewhat less dusty alternative, you may use rice or tiny lentils instead of flour (but arrange them on a tray to keep the grains generally in one spot) (but place them on a tray to keep the grains roughly in one place).

20. Play Traffic Lights

You're the traffic light and your kid is the automobile. Get them vrooming about the room. When you shout, 'Red!', they have to halt. When you say, "Green!", they can vroom off again. Later, you may introduce "Amber!" and have a quick (green) and slow (amber) pace to the vrooming.

21. Be a farmer or zookeeper

If you've got a farm or zoo set – or simply animal toys and some tiny cardboard boxes – assist your toddler to construct their animal kingdom.

Hold the animals up one by one and make the proper noises (if the animal figurines have electronic sounds, turn the off) (if the animal figures have electronic sounds, turn them off).

Talk to your child about which animal goes in which 'house' and what food they consume. And if you have a farmer figure, allow your kid to move the figure about the animals and you can chat together about what the farmer is doing for each one - combing its coat, milking it, feeding it, releasing it out into the field and so on.

22. Play Match the Socks
Unpair some various colored socks, jumble them all up and urge your youngster to match the sock pairs together by color. Or, if you don't like messing up your sock drawer (or all your socks are black!), you might get a bit inventive with this handmade 'tumble dryer' sock sorting game we discovered on YouTube.

23. Make family photo art
Print out some pics of your child and your family. Find a nice big piece of paper and some PVA glue and a spreading stick (or a glue stick) and help your child make a collage of family photos to pin up on the wall or fridge.

24. Hunt the teddy

Hide Teddy (or another favorite soft toy) somewhere in the room (where your child can reach it) and go looking for Teddy together. Perhaps Teddy will 'magically' squeak when you get near (how are your ventriloquism skills?). Older toddlers might enjoy hiding Teddy for you to find, too.

25. Play newspaper hopscotch

For this simplified version of the classic game, you'll sheets of old newspaper and some adhesive tape. Tape the newspaper sheets around the room, each of them relatively near to the other. Get your youngster to leap from one sheet to another, without hitting the floor in between.

26. Fill the cardboard box

Find a medium to the large-size cardboard box and open up the top. Place it on the floor in front of your child and encourage them how to put items in it – from toys to pillows to books. When it's almost filled, shut the top flaps, and then open them again with a flourish. Now it's time to empty the box! Your toddler could love pushing the entire box around the floor, too.

Chapter 3

Additional home-based speech therapy activities

Speech Therapy Exercises to Try at Home
Ideally, you should work with a Speech-Language Pathologist to enhance your language abilities. Then, you may utilize the following speech therapy activities to practice at home in the meanwhile.

Here are some speech therapy activities you may do at home:

1. Tongue In-and-Outs
Stick your tongue out and hold it for 2 seconds, then draw it back in. Hold for 2 seconds, then repeat. This helps educate your tongue to move in coordinated patterns, which will help you generate better speech.

2. Tongue Side-to-Side

For this speech therapy practice, open your mouth and move your tongue to contact the right corner of your mouth. Hold for 2 seconds, then touch the left corner of your lips. Hold for 2 seconds, then repeat.

3. Tongue Up-and-Down

Open your mouth and put your tongue out. Then, stretch your tongue up toward your nose. Hold for 2 seconds, then stretch your tongue down toward your chin. Hold for 2 seconds, then repeat.

It's recommended to conduct all of these speech therapy exercises in front of the mirror so that you can obtain visual feedback.

4. Say Cheese!

Here's another basic speech therapy activity that develops oral motor skills. Practice smiling in front of a mirror. Smile, then relax. Repeat as much as you can stand.

The mirror is vital because it offers feedback, which is fuel for your brain!

5. Practice Your Kissy Face
When you're done practicing those grins, try creating kissy expressions by puckering your lips. Pucker your lips together, then relax. Repeat as frequently as you can. You should slow down the movement for even greater control.

6. Consonant & Vowel Pairing Repetition
Now that we've done the easy speech therapy exercises, let's move on to more complicated tasks.

Take a consonant that you have problems speaking, and then couple it with each of the 5 vowels (a, e, I o, u) (a, e, i, o, u). For example, if you have problems with the "r" sound, then practice repeating "ra, re, ri, ro, ru" again and over.

If you're feeling adventurous, try this with all consonants.

7. Sentence Production
Patients with speech apraxia, for example, have no issue with the cognitive part of language creation. However, their capacity to move their lips and tongue is hampered.

Therefore, reading aloud gives a chance to practice speaking. This may be difficult for persons with moderate to severe aphasia, so be patient with yourself.

Start small by practicing a phrase or two for brief periods, like one or two minutes. Then, increase your practice time from there.

8. Phonological Processing
Phonology refers to the pattern of spoken sounds. Speech therapy activities that aid with phonology may help patients improve their capacity to create speech.

For this assignment, you will estimate how many syllables are in a word. Ask a caregiver to sit down with you and speak various words. Each time they pronounce a word, guess how many syllables are in that word.

Your caregiver should always inform you whether you are right or incorrect to offer feedback. The feedback is part of what makes this practice beneficial.

9. Word Games
Word games provide fantastic speech therapy exercises for adults. Although you aren't making a speech, these games stress your language processing abilities.

To focus on your visual processing and understanding, use computer games like solitaire or alchemy.

To develop your problem solving and visual processing, consider word games like word searches or crossword puzzles.

Most brain games can aid enhance speaking when you practice them consistently.

10. Speech Therapy Exercise Apps
While the exercises above are a fantastic place to start, they aren't personalized to your issue areas.

To obtain even greater outcomes, it's a wonderful idea to consider utilizing speech therapy applications like CT Speech and Cognitive Therapy App. It analyses your problem areas and recommends workouts to match your requirements.

Best of all, the CT App has hundreds of exercises so that you may obtain great treatment without the necessity of a professional. In reality, the app was built by Speech-Language Pathologists to offer better treatment for their patients at home.

While it's always better to work with a therapist, many therapists urge patients to use the CT App at home between appointments.

11. Read books with your youngster
Even when they are newborns. Reading aloud age-appropriate books while simultaneously discussing the graphics will attract their interest. While you name items in the book, the youngster will have visual help.
This may promote learning new terms. Similar to signing, reading books aloud enhances the child's vocabulary.

Chapter4

Increasing effectiveness

There are various ways speech therapy may help a child's communication and cognitive development, even if they haven't yet uttered their first word. In this article, we discuss the various advantages of speech therapy for toddlers and young children.

There are several reasons why babies and toddlers, even beginning as early as three months old, might benefit from speech therapy.

Language development starts in early life far before a youngster begins creating their first words. Crying, babbling, pointing, and gesturing are all aspects of early language acquisition, and they represent a child's initial efforts to convey their ideas, emotions, and wishes.

Children who are non-verbal must nonetheless be able to successfully communicate. Not only is this vital as kids begin to perceive the world around them, but it helps create the framework for speech production, connection building, social awareness, and literacy abilities like reading and writing.

How Speech Therapy Can Improve a Toddler's Communication Beyond Just Speech?

When we think of speech therapy, the first thing that comes to mind is frequently verbal communication, such as speaking or pronouncing sounds properly. However, speech therapy is considerably broader and encompasses language comprehension, social skills, and all areas of oral and writing communication.

Speech therapy may develop several communication skills needed for newborns and young children beyond simply speech. These include:

- Non-Verbal Communication

Speech therapy may assist newborns and toddlers with the most fundamental types of communication. This may involve the use of gestures or facial expressions, as well as basic noises to convey their needs and wishes even before they're ready to utilize words or entire phrases. When young children fail to convey their thoughts, they may also be more prone to behavioral disorders. By establishing a firm foundation of language, speech therapy may help young children develop and flourish into competent communicators.

- Social communication

At this early age, children are starting to build bonds and emotional ties. Unfortunately, social skills don't come effortlessly to all youngsters, which may be worsened once they attend school and begin associating with others. Speech therapy focuses on social development through exercises such as matching emotions to facial expressions, identifying body language and social cues, teaching turn-taking, practicing how to follow directions, interacting with people in a variety of different settings, and for older children, working on conversational skills.

- Cognitive Development

Even when a kid is born, until approximately age five, their brains are actively growing. A child's cognitive talents touch so many elements of their everyday life, including their working memory, reasoning, and problem-solving skills, self-awareness, executive functioning, understanding, motivation, and more. Strong language and communication skills are crucial to increasing cognitive function and nurturing healthy, autonomous children.

- Foundational Literacy Skills

Reading, writing, and spelling are all language-based activities. As noted, a good foundation in the language is required to increase reading abilities and flourish academically. More precisely, early language development helps toddlers acquire phonological awareness (the capacity to distinguish distinct sounds within a word), which they subsequently use to transfer related sounds onto written words.

This ability is crucial to helping children become excellent readers and is the building block for spelling, writing, and comprehension to ensure they absorb and comprehend what they read.

How Do I Know My Toddler Needs Speech Therapy?

Not that we've proven the breadth of speech therapy goes much beyond speaking, let's concentrate on signals that your young kid might benefit from assistance. It's crucial to recognize that all children are distinct and follow their growth path. Just because your kid isn't demonstrating certain habits doesn't always imply they won't ultimately catch up. However, if you do discover your kid isn't achieving milestones suitable for their age, you should consider discussing it with your doctor or requesting an examination from a qualified speech therapist.

- 0-12 month milestones

Not of Smiling or Noticing Those: Early in a child's infancy, at approximately the three-month mark, youngsters begin paying attention to others around them. Your youngster should begin smiling or responding while you're chatting to them.
Making Baby Noises: The lovely baby gaggles begin after a few months of existence. This is when toddlers begin exploring with their vocal cords and

generating a range of various sounds. Even if they're far from creating a readable speech, infants should be making noises often throughout the day.

- 12 - 18 month milestones

First Words: Around this age, it's normal that newborns begin to pronounce their first words. These words generally start simply like "mamma" or "baba."
12 - 24 month milestones

Simple Phrases: Putting simple words together to make comprehensible phrases is a significant communication milestone. Don't anticipate complete phrases at this age, but, your kid should be able to offer a clearer indication of their requirements. For example, kids should say "I want" while pointing to the juice, or "more milk" if they're still hungry.

- 24 - 36 month milestones

Pronouncing Sounds and Words: There are common sounds that are tougher for youngsters to learn, such as the /ch/ or /l/ sound. However, by age 3 children should be able to coherently make several sounds, and be comprehensible at least 75 percent of the time to both known and new listeners. Additionally, a child's speech should be understandable by those they often engage with, including family members or close friends.

Playing with Others: Children at this age begin to often play and mingle with others their age. This is when their social abilities truly emerge, and we begin to observe the development of other crucial early language skills, including turn-taking and following instructions. While some children are naturally timid, this may frequently be mistaken as a child's inability to grasp people or make themselves known.

Online Speech Therapy for Toddlers
Many toddlers and young children not only appreciate online speech therapy, but it may also assist speed their growth and communication milestones.

Made in the USA
Monee, IL
27 November 2022

18689977R00036